Sometimes the Little Town

An Homage to Elkton, Virginia

Poetry by
Sara M. Robinson

Sometimes the Little Town

Cedar Creek Publishing
Bremo Bluff, Virginia
www.cedarcreekauthors.com

Printed in the United States of America
Library of Congress Control Number 2016931548
ISBN 978-1-942882-04-6

Acknowledgements

For her never-ending faith in my writing and her understanding
of my need to do so, my never-ending love to Carolyn.

For her generous support of my poetry and her courage
to edit my writing, my gratitude to Grace Zisk.

For Mark Collins, who finds depth in my writing and
challenges me to keep improving and keep writing.

For their support and feedback when I submitted them to
various drafts of my poems, my sincere thanks to Paul, Don, Burt,
Barbara, Laura, Addison, Shirley, Gene, Joyce, Richard, and Trish.

And, about six years ago, in a little town's community center, Linda Layne patiently and
willingly listened to me speak of my town and my book plans. She encouraged me to
write about it; and through her support my efforts now bring notice to Elkton and to Hobby.
With much thanks and appreciation, I can't give enough credit to her.

———————————————

The poem, "Leaving Elkton," first appeared in
Two Little Girls in a Wading Pool (Cedar Creek Publishing, 2012).

The poem, "Sometimes the Little Town," first appeared in
the 2015 issue of *The Virginia Literary Journal.*

All photos are from the collection and estate of Hobby Robinson
and have appeared in his previously-published books. Copyright protected.

Hobby Robinson books:
Every One Means Something to Someone (two editions); *So Many of Them; Bless Them All;
Nine to Ninety; Mish Mash; Apron Strings; Across the Alley; Welcome to Our World.*

Dedication

To Hobby Robinson, my father –
As he would say in his books, "This one's for you."

I look out beyond valleys and over your majestic shoulders.
The little girl I am sees her future and wants so much
to tell it, someday, but first she must leave her town.

Then she must come back and see it again and again
through your eyes, Dad. I pretend now I am the camera.

And, to my Elkton-born or -raised friends and cousins,
I submit my poetry filled with love
and enormous tenderness for you all.

TABLE OF CONTENTS

Introduction

Hobby Robinson was one of the most important photographers of the 20th century to be so little well-known, at least outside the Shenandoah Valley of central Virginia. He chronicled over three generations of Elkton townsfolk, compiling and self-publishing nine books. Using his vast collection of photographs, his own and those he obtained, he gave us a people and a place. His anecdotes and quips of history are hilarious and heart-wrenching; perfect fodder for me, as poet, to use as inspiration. Today these books are hard to find, with complete sets just about impossible to have.

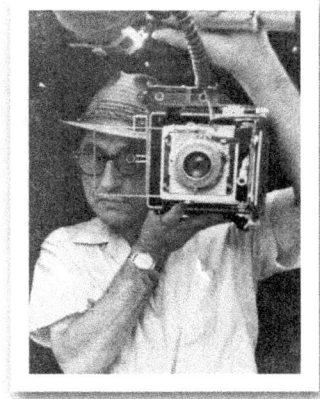

I want him to be remembered and I want our town to be noticed and appreciated like all small towns should be. I hope my poetry book, bringing his work back to life in another way, will inspire others to do the same. Our town is every town. Every other town is part of a bigger world.

The large is ever present in the small.

Unlike my earlier poetry books, where I only had a few or so Elkton-focused poems, in this collection, I get to devote the entire book to Elkton's people (and a couple of buildings). I hope you enjoy meeting them all. They are, here or gone from us, truly wonderful.

Sara M. Robinson

Sometimes the Little Town

*So I find words I never thought to speak/In streets I never thought I should revisit/
When I left my body on a distant shore.* — T. S. Eliot

I

Comes the valley in winter
where frost lies in wait
and the town angles in
its repose. The sleepiness
of the buildings overflows
into the habits of those
generations who've lived
surrounded by much that is
not moving. The sun rising
over nearby mountains glances
off the middling creek rushing
to the grand Shenandoah now
frozen on its edges. Sap of old
spirits flows through the center
in water moving fast to leave the
town and makes its way to the
bigger river, then on to a distant sea.

No prospects for spring jump out at
this moment. No blossom evidence
or awakening creatures greet anyone
on these cold mornings. No one can yet
detect a spring aroma. Unless you count
the memory of young locust wood
in remains airborne from home fireplaces.

If you drive across the river and
find your way into town, you might
glance in your rear-view mirror and see
what you have left. Your GPS doesn't work

backwards so just turn it off. You can see
time and distance receding, separate from
space as it changes with each mile you
drive forward. If you drive into town you
might notice old buildings still standing,
guarding the past. Crumbling façades cling to
sidings like faded make-up on old movie stars.
A few might have transitioned to more
recent times but they would be anomalies—
themselves better relics than the old ones.

How picturesque and yet sad
for this little town in the valley.

Your travels have brought you here
not to document or study any history.
That has been done. You are here to see
the dead, those buried in the cemetery
where resting among so many others
no one speaks–especially not the living.
For what would you say, but that you were
passing through and thought you might look
upon names of former residents. Some are your
kin, some are friends, many are strangers, yet
they all will speak to you in ways you cannot
hear, but can feel. The language may be buried
but it talks through your skin. You wander among
the gravesites, pick here and there at hobo weeds,
robbing them of their trespass while you proceed
with yours in this little cemetery in this little town,
where you will not be buried but where you
will always reside. It is in your mind; and within
the crevices and folds of your brain, memories
will repose until you or some dead ghost nudges
them awake. The rattling will tell you when.

II

Along the sidewalks in concrete gutters
and buried main lines, particles of the past
meet particles of the present
and neither recognizes the other.
These are remains of fires
which burnt down the town
at the first turn of the twentieth
century. Blazes seen across the
valley and from mountain ridges
took everything in their ravenous
destined march of destruction.
People grieved for properties lost
and cried in relief for bodies saved.
They would rebuild on this very soil,
still covered with ashes. Burnt as the
ground was, the char was either swept
away or was blended into the mortar
holding tight the new foundations.
Trees were planted, roads recast over
remains of thoroughfares. Birds
returned along with residents and hands
worn to blisters at the end of each day
had enough tenderness left to touch a
salvaged water pitcher or a sunburned cheek.

When I see old pictures of those times
I think of all the people in their
black suits and black dresses
milling about the remains. I wish
I could see what they thought. I wish I
could feel their grief. I wish I
could believe in their hope.

They did not take up their resurrection
work in vain. Whether they thought future

generations would know of their
efforts I cannot say. But I believe they
did. Why else build? Why were
they there? They would not rebuild for the
dead. They built for the living,
for those in the future. For me. For you.

III

When I return to the streets whose names and
numbers I cannot recall, I feel this past come
up through my feet and into my heart. To attempt
to tell a stranger of my town would
be recognizing my own journey between
the two places that define me. I would need a
new language filled with words from my past
conjugated within the words that I speak now.
To carefully merge these two worlds would be
practicing syntax I once discarded and now must
recover. That is why I am here. That is why
I write about this little town in the valley.

The town, it grew and prospered in my youth.
Among the merchants was our family store
where settlers and farmers came in to purchase
and to barter. In the fall, baskets of southern yams
would appear from wagons in hopes of trades
for school shoes and Sunday-best shirts. Smoked
hams came out of tired and worn burlap sacks as
currency for ladies' dresses and hats. Jars of pickles
and canned tomatoes were stacked on our counter
like casino winnings. We thrived on wooden
buckets of late summer beans and corn, headed
for the big pot on our stove. Like the other
merchants, we believed we were rich having been
given earth-born coins far greater than gold
ones as these contained the rewards for labor

from neighbors and friends who formed the
true character of our little town in the valley.

We all made do with what we had. We may have
lacked some of the cultural assumptions of a
larger place but we had the purity of a culture
formed from dust, honeysuckle, blackberries,
mudpuppies, corn rows, arrowheads, musket balls,
milk buckets, coarse woolen yarns and naked creeks.
We called this town our beginning and our end.
We took leaving to heart even when we left
for just a day or a few hours. When we left for
what we thought was for good we took some of
the town with us. We might find it later as some
old mud stuck on a shoe or a discovered letter
from an old friend, but these elements were our bond.

IV

I'm on a trampoline where all the years of my life
have been stenciled. I watch my ages bounce off one number
and boomerang back to another. When I jump up,
I don't look down. When I land I'm instantly that age, but
I cannot stay. I either have to keep moving or jumping.
No matter what, the ages still catch up with me and all I can do
is wear the years like costume jewelry, that either sparkles in
the light, or simply fizzles out. My aging creased skin is my façade
and my hair is the glowing reminder of how
our past can burn white hot.

V

We talk to the dead in our town and we listen for their replies.
We know they have departed and yet we still talk to them
as if we think they will return to us. We are a town with a
history and I am part of this history. My redemption
will only come in time when I find that I measure my life

in moments. My history will rapidly come full circle
and I will return to reside in this last place
on earth. The river will run swiftly around me,
pulling against the gravity of my past as it competes

with the gravity of my present. My ashes will come
ashore and mingle with the long gone ashes used to
rebuild. In a winter whirl of time someone may
remember the town's beginning and recite it as
what remains of me swirls in the purest water
on earth that nurtured my little town in the valley.

Philosophy According to John

Who are our philosophers, John?
When did they speak to you,
in low voices rising from creek beds

or perhaps from the floors of our
town stores? Did they tell you to
go and speak great truths? To us,

what was it you were supposed to say?
New oracles of places yet to be seen.
Maybe you would share some

of this wisdom with us. Or must we pry
the truth from your gentle hands as if
we were thirsting to know.

John Gochenour

Tannery Men, ca. 1912

Likely it was no accident
men assembled on a summer
day for a picture. It is quiet.

No one speaks or smiles.
They are not sure what
the picture will mean. Perhaps

a documentation of one
day's toil or an accounting
of who was present that

particular day when rough
necks and shirts coupled
with mustaches and skin.

In other countries they
might be mistaken for
Mexican border bandits.

But with faces thinned by
exposure to acid, worry,
and some sorrow, they find

a rest from the hides,
to meet under a large
oak. Black ones and

white ones standing
still, looking right at
the photographer,

who was adjusting
his films and focus:
a start of some history.

Tannery Crew about 1912

Field Day, 1908

Find a man or woman:
any good man or woman
set them in the village
amongst flowers and curbs.

Watch as they parade through
stores and dwell in company
of their choosing. These are
the folks we know and these
are the ones who last after
sunset in long shadows
of purity on horizon's edge.

In My Home

I wrote their stories in my government-issue records book.
Inside water-stained family bibles, proof of

their truths penciled in archaic script bore witness. I took
them at their word. I knew this was hard. I had to note each

member as part of their resettlement from the mountains.
They could not take transplants of their prized laurel

or ginseng with them. Only their bodies would leave—
their spirits and their ghosts would remain on the slopes.

Now I stand here before you a man who has seen much
including suffering. The lines on my face, these indentations

of my life are merged with theirs. We are not separate
and I know we breathe the same air.

My children and their children and so on will know someday
that while I saw changes I felt the steadfastness of place.

I wept sometimes for what I wrote but still I wrote.
We all yearn for home.

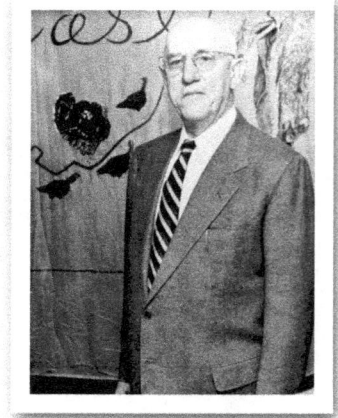

C. C. Housh, Sr.

A Good Look at Life

I've listened to a thousand stories.
Most of them are mine and when I think
of this great America I recall the best
of this town. I talk from my heart and I say
I am of this town and all that I can hold
is this town.

I can travel away from this town. But I won't.
I can ride to the edges where pasture meets the
mountain and streams meet the lawns. All these

wonderful things I can see from the lawn chair
on my porch among iris blossoms. I can speak
to anyone I meet. If I left for America I would miss

too much here. If I left my town and my beloved
home, what would I have, but a memory? I
need more than that: I need the ground. My family
is from valley clay and my blood is the river.

I can take only what I can hold in my eyes.
I am not so tired to see what you see, too.

Charlie Powell

The Oak is a Big Deal

I am of the Bur Oak:
our grand tree which
suffers many blows
but does not fall.

Crowd me not
with lesser species
but love me more
with gentler spirits.

Caress me with spring
tassels as I smile
knowing what I know
and doing what I do.

Jesse Deal

Clothes Define Us

Good money was paid for that suit,
the dark gray that he wore for the
one formal photograph ever to be
taken. He saved a week's pay for

the barber who groomed his mustache
and his black wavy hair to the
perfection desired for such an important
pose. His serious face with just
a light hint of self-satisfaction did

him proud with the sublime
justice that he deserved. Will
he stand again as he did in the
picture? Will he give us once
more a chance to love him?
There are so few gentlemen

and he would be so welcomed
in our parlor where we could hang
his coat and brush his shoes. A
quick once-over just as the moment
ends and we have to go back to
before: before there was that suit.

Epp Eaton

I Stay With Earth

For what will I rule in my life
to be content?
How shall I make my home
within granaries or silos?

I wave my hand over
golden grasses and I see
all of my heirs as well as
all of my friends.

I am content as one
of the land for what
it has given me.
Grains to wheat,
wheat to bread,
bread for life
When I mill I find the earth.

I stay here.

Ed Louderback

What's in a Name?

From where did this name begin
was as much a mystery as one
who stands in snow with brand-
new bib overalls to have his
picture taken for what reason.

The whys and hows may elude
us but still we know journeys
taken under different names
would still continue, would they not?

Places and names come apart in
small towns like the slow unfolding
of a mysterious origami puzzle.

W. Baugher (Billy Tanat)

A Storied Life

Tuxedoed in my own
formality witness this:
I have walked this town.
I have not gone far but
I have seen those who
live here within the
serenity of a small town
are not disturbed
by any ghosts of the past.

They hold the dignity that
becomes streets themselves,
which border the façades
of houses in which all
truths are either revealed
or hidden. But neither
matters for we are still

the ones who stayed here.
When we walk over
our grassy lawns or through
our willowy fields, we can
still feel the spirits of those
who came before, but did not leave.

Reese Cover

Limestone Binds Water

We stand posed, defiant, or
were we just stern as we
supposed we should be
for a memorable photo.

We are rockbound with
limestone that caught
us hundreds of years ago.

We have a purpose: we
are all of you and you
are all of us and though
you keep trying to leave,

we find you and
bring you back.

Sam and George Baugher

Little Beaver Lives Big

Much is told of the scant exhibition
 of life measured in such stature taking
small steps and many of them at that.

His life was fuller than most who are
three times his size and height.
And he could dance better than
those who bragged of better
position, but ran out of buffoonery.

Give me the friendly voice and
manly spirit of this small
man, who in his existence was
the very essence of the town,
the life force of those who could
dream big and stay firmly planted.

Henry "Shorty" Stepp

The Ship That Was So Grand

"Had he known what it was to be flush"*

he might have taken a larger swallow of
the bitter-sweet liquor before saying his vows.

With soon-learned characteristic bravado he
presented himself as a future son-in-law.

With this announcement and with that pride
he set upon the family as the one who
readily gambled for coins of the realm,

one who was not concerned with loss
but easily embraced the art of gain.
He was a magnificent ship.

*Walt Whitman

Kenny Davis

An Ordinary Chair

He sits in the chair
as if he was assembled
within the slats as it was
put together.

Arms relaxed, crossed,
one hand with a cigarette.
A new pencil in his pocket
signals he has work to do
later. But for now he's

content to face the camera.
He takes in the whole world
and he realizes he is equal
to all surrounding him.

He will give up all his
knowledge in return for
what he has learned
in just a few lines:
he is one with the earth
and his earth is one with him.

Maynard Downey

Adored

O, Elkton: I want to keep you
in your ancient besieged state.
Trapped like old muskrats, we are.
Too placid and too stubborn
to move away.
Dug in along the run and intoxicated
by the river we do not leave.
I want you to stay in that state
where I can adore you.

F. P. Hammers

Camera Obscura

There is a town that is no more a town
surrounded by farms that are no more farms
with roads that are no more roads that lead
there but mostly lead away.

The town is a story found in books about it
with pictures that will break your heart by
a photographer who broke many hearts with
his cool detachment hidden beneath his camera.

He loved as none in this town
have ever loved. He shot, developed, and
cropped buildings into geolithic structures
built right into the ground where most remain
to this day empty and barren not unlike
stray moons one can see from
time to time in a just-as-lonely sky.

You could put this town, like a sailing ship,
inside a clear bottle and place it up on a mantle
where guests could peer inside and pretend
they knew all the streets and people. Nothing
would be moving, trapped like the ship. It is just
a display after all. You could break it with
a hammer, watch pieces fly out, sift through
remains, then wonder if you should
try to put it all back together again.

We can't see inside the town to find people
moving in and out of their day nor can we
see a night sky bursting with stars filling
up from edge to edge. We would be better
served with a big nightlight that can light
up all the hallways in all the houses in
the town that is no more a town. Within

our imagination and memories we can shapeshift anything we want. There is no dearth of bottles; and like the cosmos filled with its mysteries the town retains its own singularity. We can only peer on the edge and wonder what would happen if we were to fall over. See the people.

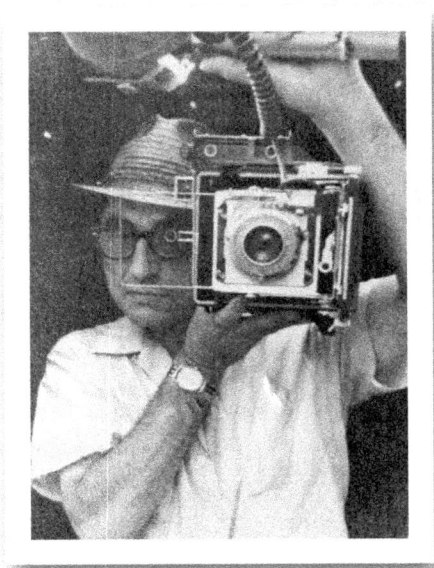

Hobby Robinson

The Town Speaks by the River

The dwelling starts with those
within and those without. We
take hold of timbers and
braces with sturdy hands
and willing backs. Our stories
will emerge and unfold in
lines, phrases, and grateful
pauses. We are the underpinning
of this town and our very breaths
hold the precious air between
us and our mountains.

When you see each of us in
our moments will you see our
hands clasped together or
will our hands hold our young
or those of others?
In our suits we reveal how
serious our lives are in
life and in death. We go nowhere
but we are everywhere. We speak
in new ways and in our voices
you will hear our poetry.

The words are simple, really.
They reveal us in our captivity
bound with shackles
of wheat straw and drinking
river water of clearest taste and
hints of freedom in its rapids.

Love Among Wools and Flannels

Before she was the wife,
before she was the mother
she grew up in the small town
amidst the packaged shirts and
hand-tailored trousers. The men
in her life fashioned themselves
as the local clothing gentry and
gave her the tools to someday
take their trade and make a
grand bargain.

When he first appeared, a short
stocky Russian with a neatly
pressed suit, she was told he
had come with honorable
intentions—but he hoped to
win her heart as none before
had ever done. He could speak
the language of wools, gabardines,
eastern European poets. With
his letters of earnest devotion

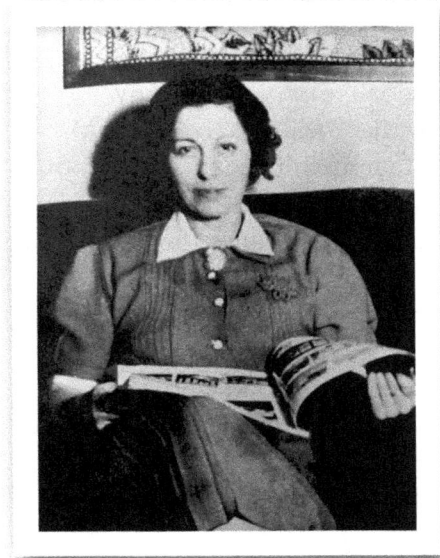

Mrs. Sadye Robinson
(Mother of Hobby Robinson)

he won her heart and then
the store, the beginning of
his humanity with the town,
and the fulfillment of all
that would follow. In their
newness of wedding and
commitment, they did not
know someday their son
and his daughter would pull all
this together in more than black
and white, more than just still life,
more than his love for them; it would

be the history of everything.

EHS Pinafore

Suppose fourteen teenage women
decided to organize into a
basketball team. They already
knew that their dress code would
dictate something long, dark, wool,
and perhaps a little on the severe
side. They were ladies after all.

So the decision was black wool
with sailor ties and bows in front
accented with "E" in whitewash
so it could be easily removed if
desired. They could wear their
hair high and back off the forehead
as befitting young women who
wanted to look winsome, lovely,
and serious all at the same time.

They pulled it off. Their expressions
of surprise, pleasure, serenity,
and determination were conveyed
properly with the utmost in decorum
which was no small task as the wait
for the shutter to trip was a long one,
and these were young girls, eager
to jump up (with grace and dignity
you understand) and bounce
that old leather ball to the basket
which was their future.

The Beauties
Elkton High School Basketball Team, 1909

Your Moments of Glad Grace

If Yeats could have described
your peaceful pose with the camera.
If he could have read your mind,
he would have known your inner
soul and touched a heart fed
by the very flowers whose scent
flew into the arms of those who
often walked onto your wide porch.

Your sweetness was lavished on
many a small boy and young girl
who played among your boxwoods
and hid behind your lilacs, hoping
to see you arrive in the big black
sedan always kept shiny and ready

for trips on the small roads in
an even smaller town. Somehow
our buildings must have looked
a little grander through the lenses
of your proper pince-nez frames
so delicately balanced on your
pristine skin, made even more
reverential, surrounded (I'm
quite sure), by the rarest of pearls
and your styled silver hair.

To know that your beauty was
nourished by our mountain spring
water and our own native produce
made us all the richer in your glow.

Mrs. I. L. Flory

Secrets Hidden From View

(On the lament of having
her photo taken by her
loving husband):

Your eyes said, hurry up,
and get this over with.
Your pursed lips spoke
in silence of your discomfort.

Yet surrounded by your sons
and daughters you knew
your husband would frame
this experience in one loud

click of the shutter and the
instant spark of the large
sulfur strip. You didn't even
blink, but your hands gave

away your secret. The one
you would tell your grandson
the next day. He promised
not to give it up, but then

he saw you smile and he saw
his grandfather smile and
he knew this would be
better than any treasure

he had hidden under the
front porch.

Mrs. F. P. Hammers

It's Always Missing a Candle

At what age do we say:
    no more photos?
I can't imagine giving up
the chance to celebrate
the one day that validates
all the other days.

More than birth of twin sons.
More than when I finished my
beloved tatted shawl, a treasure
which keeps me warm.

I sit here.   My long life
behind me   telling you
who has given me
the archive of this one day
that I am ready now.

    I am ready for this picture.

    And the next day.

Mrs. Herring

Song in the Key of Companionship

Mothers-in-law, faithful friends
who watched their son and daughter
build lives and forge families during
one Christmas time when this
picture was taken, had been talking
about how Spring would be so
welcome after all the snow.

Warmed by the living room stove
they posed by the piano where
many times they had listened to
grandchildren and nieces sing the
adored hymns that never failed

to give them warmth and comfort.

Mrs. Lough and Mrs. Dyche

I sing verses and speak of their
companionship as if I were sitting
there with them, but I wasn't.
While I did not know at the time
that my grandmother would die
in just a few months, I can hear
their smiles and I can see in their
faces that sorrow will flee and

joy will rise up as the herald of
a good life. They speak to me:
we have filled our hearts with
devotion and adoration for our
families and our faith though
there is plenty of room for the
world. There is plenty for

we dwell in quiet grandeurs.

New Hampshire

She bottle-feeds the baby pig.
Jacketed, wearing her everyday
apron she has stopped for the
camera. It's winter and in a
January weather break the
hogs have produced their litters.

But she nurses one—this one
she'll keep as she has named
the little female, Willie.

Sometimes on a farm one
remembers that giving and
taking lives is a gift and
a chore. There are those
considered lesser which must
be given up to feed the larger.

Then there is the one little
pig that drinks the cow's milk
and grunts with pleasure causing
a big smile from one who knows

there will be no harvesting today.

Mrs. Willie Davis

Your Eyes Which Gazed So Confidently

To say you were impeccable would be
an insult to the extraordinary demeanor
which you carried like a proud civil
rights worker except this picture was
taken long before women rose up to
establish their bona fides in this country.

You were the grandest, the smartest, the
savviest, the proudest of any of our
women and we all wanted to be like you.
We all wanted to be you, but courage
is a special trait that only a few can carry.

Stationed in life, you had the confidence
of one who has seen much and yet remained
convinced there was much more to be seen
and experienced. How you did this was
part of your mystery but as I see
how you are dressed, how immaculate
your attire and how relaxed you are

Helen Corman - Aunt Helen

in this pose, I know there were sparks
of many fires simmering within and
when I heard of your adventures, your
next conquests, I wasn't surprised
to learn that you dazzled them all and
left nations of men to marvel at how great it
felt to be conquered.

The Rarity of Splendor

There was nothing earth-bound for her.

There was no silk yet to be spun.
No thread yet to be dyed.
No wool soon to be sheared.

No grass yet to be greened.
No tree left to be leafed.
No river yet to be flowed.

Skyward, no bird yet to be flown
except for one feathered majestic canary
who lifted with chiffon wings from
earth, yet to be fully grown,

and took our hearts—our broken hearts—
with her. The sky, devoid of words,
is an empty nest.

Lee DeArmond

You Are Your Name

Eight names to make one name. A name
so long it needed coordinates defined by
longitude and latitude to be properly
recognized and given its proper estate.

A name which could have been described
by numerical units of acreage. Hectares
would be sufficient but not nearly as
memorable as a Gladys or an Elizabeth
or an Ellen or an Evangeline. And in
this sentence of a name, which yet here

remains unfinished, the insertion of
Thistledown brings forth an ancient
living record of some far off place
anchored by Dyche, then Bruce, lastly
Ruebush providing safe harbors in

a little valley residing between
named mountains where rivers and
creeks, also named, carry the names
of fishes and lesser animals whose
names while not as long as hers,
bear all the distinction of having a name.

So, in nineteen syllables we have been
given a singular person who now gives
back to us a chance to recall how each
of us when we speak our names should
be clear, complete, unafraid.

Gladys Elizabeth Ellen
Evangeline Thistledown Dyche
Bruce Ruebush

Incalculable Beauty

Is there no measure in science,
no rhyme pattern or poetic
acuity worthy of her?

How naïve of me to think
I would grasp in brief lines
the perfection she unveils
in the mere placement of her
hands. Then there is sublime

triumph of tender curiosity in
her eyes as she's about to ask
a question to which we would
give millions to know the answer.

Thelma C. Heatwole

When Legends Begin

She sat right down,
lightly brushed dust
off her mauve cotton
dress and smiled. Fresh
from hanging out baseball
socks, her face almost
gave way to laughter,
the pure joy of knowing
one of her boys had just
hit the long ball out of
the cow pasture ball park.
The dust still rises.

Nannie Monger Dofflemeyer

When Life is a Surprise

Toward whom or what
do you sight your young
dark eyes curious in a

    bemused sort of way?

You hold on to your youngster
(tempted to smile) but
you know you are keeping

    a thunderbolt from escaping

out of the picture, the one
that had to be taken on this
cold day when you promised

    a kitten as a reward and

said tabby appears off in
the trees. Now the child
wants to flee from you

    determined for the surprise.

But this is life today when there
will be time enough to come:
bringing in longer days, clear nights,

    and we have smelled Spring.

Mrs. W. E. Kite
and daughter, Mary Elizabeth

Still Life with Virginia

How so Virginia, so country
Miss Lena is. How rooted—
how grand she must be

to let her picture be taken
beside a very shiny milk cow.
It is possible no words

can be found for such
as this. A farm woman
faces the camera.

The cow chews on grass
and there is the heavy pail
which may be filled or not—

But with such a rich life,
let's say it's at least half.

Mrs. Lena Blose

When We Watch From Our Porches

We may not know the richness of poverty
nor the indigence of richness—for how would
we attempt to explain how a front porch
defines one's station in life. We have
a porch outside the kitchen door so
we can churn milk in the afternoon breeze.

We have the porch outside the front door
so we can receive guests and assemble
for family portraits. It's the cleanest.

We have our porch so on Saturday nights
we can watch fireflies create brief movies
on our dirt-spattered front yards. From our

Mrs. Tom Monger

porch we can call up the youngsters to have
their picture taken by the traveling photographer
who has slicked down the boys' hair and knocked
a bit of mud off their shoes and overalls.

He poses their mom with the new twins in her
special rolling chair and pleads with them to
be ready when he yells smile. But she is weary
and while this is her best dress: it is the only one
she has that can be used for an occasion other

than Sunday. She squints at him because she
must get dinner ready and the cookstove is
unattended. Fatback burns fast and creasies
will scorch. There will be no biscuits tonight.

Monarchs Feed on Milkweed Wild in Fields

You don't ever have to leave this place. This town's
siren call keeps you tied to its invisible mast
even if you try to ignore the pleas to stay, and even
if the love songs
                torture the very interior of you,

you cannot continue to breathe the air or drink the water
it is too magical and too consuming. If you want to breathe
underwater someday and migrate hundreds of miles then
                you must break the magic.

Your life will take on numerous journeys and in every one
you will feel the town. It is too rooted in your own private
interior. You can feel the darkness on days that are
                too sunny to see.

You can feel the chill on days that are too
heated to survive. You can feel the sky overhead on
winds blowing too strongly for you to remain upright.

Look all around you as you leave. You can see gates
swing open and shut from almost every direction. You
can hear ungreased hinges creaking. You can feel
hot breaths rise from the road and from the cemetery.
                You drive on streets that never change.

You won't come back and you won't go. The maze has no
beginning and no ending. You keep finding new bits of
your past and you peck only at pieces you can
swallow, pack quickly in a spot that won't show. Your
travels are circular but your life is a straight line,
                sometimes hidden under mud.

Cockscomb

In its privileged spot
parading its privileged stride
the cock of the rock tells
lies on the innocent.

And in the irony that every
yard boasted of this brilliant
braggadocio no one cared
who was innocent or guilty,
nor of what anyone could be.

The lights went on at dusk,
people came inside from day's
labors and found positions
comfortable for telling

their stories, stopping only
to drink from the spring's
pure gift or even from the town's
own which filtered slowly down
from falls hidden within cedars.

All water here runs clean
and clear and if such currents
could be patient, then slowly
set the pace for those histories
to unfold, perhaps we would

see the sweet williams grow
from the rocks weathered
smooth and the dirt weathered
black, rich, and bold, filled with
those stories of who we are.

He Can Repair Anything

Could repair anything they all said.
Made his own guitars so we heard,
but then we never heard him play
one of his masterpieces.
Sometimes treasures leave us
and we wonder what have we missed.

Like when someone strums a very
sad song while sitting on a broken-
down porch and no one knows who
wrote it, and we may never hear it
again exactly in that same way.

Like when one old man sits on a
diner stool, nursing a cup of java,
glances at the camera, wondering
why me, what's so special about me?

No two days are ever the same and
it makes no sense to look.

Ronda "Huey" Cave

Life is Peachy

It takes a real man—
a smiling real man
to wear plaid shorts
with an unmatched
plaid shirt lazily suited
to the neck and the day,

who can smile at a camera
and say if this picture doesn't
work, I'll stand for another.

Peachy Shifflett

Spoken Like Regular Folk

What is a native tongue? What
can we call what we speak
in our town that when one
comes here and puts down
roots he will begin to talk
in the same way? We have
what all want in such a place:
the language of rural ways,
the greetings that feel like
summer peaches carrying
warmth and sweetness.

He tempered his speech
sometimes with a gruffness
that mystified and intrigued
us when we sat at the counter
waiting for our cokes.
His larger-than-life stature
hid well his one big secret:
a heart that spoke steadily
for and loved our town.

Tom McGinnis

Family Ties

Inexplicable bounty born of desire,
risen through love and expressed
as beauty, seen in easy smiles, with
a man's eyes. Yes, too, a father's pride
of progeny not lost on us.

Such a man was not sore at the world
nor did he have but few regrets bound by time,
as he watched girls to women grow.

Such ways that would folly others
did not follow him—he had seen
birth and death—and wasted nothing.

Hillman Levinson and his six daughters

Capture

What was his handsomeness
to those who infiltrated his
hemisphere?
Was it his broad smile or his
William Powell (we can assume
no relation, such a shame) good
looks?
Maybe his sweetness for the ladies
oozed out like rising bulbs in
warmed spring soil.
All the light rises, too. And again
and again, we're captive.

Maude Lough and Alfred Powell

The Dean of Wood

I sit among fallen oaks
and severed hickories with
their blood no longer flowing.
I smell their remains—sawed
limbs and truncated midsections.

I know some things are meant to
leave us. Some things remain to
ground us. I do not weep for those
which I have cut as I am a man
from wood and I thank each and
every one with the songs of my
cross saw. My labors do not go

unrewarded. I'll remember the
fierceness of the oak come next
winter when it sparks back the
story of its life as it warms mine.

Oliver Dean

Meadows Are For Flowers

When the clan gathers no one speaks until
the mother gives the nod which can barely
be seen except by the father who will give
the word and then, only then, can anyone
smile or utter a sound. They are so still.

The young in white will stand back of
the old women in black with those younger
women in blue bordered by the men
who in gray take this gathering with
the utmost seriousness. They do not move.

Men and women know of obedience as it
is sewn into their eyes alongside stitches
of duty and faith. These will be passed on
whether they leave the mountains or stay—
destiny predetermined for them like the
ironweed and honesty which know their place
in river valleys. They move yet they remain.

The Meadows Clan

Happiness is a Six Letter Name

He smiled and for an instant light filled
up the world and burst off the page.

Brighter than a summer comet crossing
over a dark sky he shared his glee as if

it were an intoxicating perfume, unbottled,
escaping for all to breathe in. We, too,

could be intoxicated with so much happiness
to flow from: our mouths   our eyes. Mad

in a wonderful way. Such embrace we must
keep forever. We must not let Walter go.

Walter Breeden

Chiefs

As our heroes who can soar
rise to incredible heights,
we give much thanks for
time they spent here before
flight. Where do they belong
these past falcons whose kindly
eyes were not warped by misplaced
notions of human frailties, but
whose eyes gazed on many and
remembered their humanity?

Guns resting in holsters under
controlled contentment can be
noiseless, but all the more
powerful in such silence.

Walter Norvelle

The Father Remembers His Daughter
Long After They Both Are Gone

What's in a name, anyway? Could have changed mine, but didn't.
She could. She did. Never mind, Patsy. When she came to visit
I knew who she was. Told her where I was from. Sure,
I was just a blacksmith. Could hammer out an iron tune
as good as the next guy. Can't sing any better than that, I told her.

We all come from some village.
Houses sit at the foot of mountains;
when it is dark they all look alike. Houses are framed
around people. Both have to hold families up.
Lose one. Lose everything.

A child arrives. A beauty. Her voice appears just as natural as if
it was always there. Hidden. Someone will leave. But later
many will arrive. Stay. Some will fly. One will not land.

Sam Hensley (father of Patsy Cline)

Just Whistle (You Know How to Whistle, Don't You?)

if you see the enemy coming over the far ridge hauling
their shiny cannons looking for the front line. Give us time
to retreat to our soggy stinky trenches. Better to be there

with socks getting soaked taking a chance on fungus than
to be sprawled among the dead men, horses, dogs, and
whatever else remains before a truce is called.

Yeah, better to retreat into a future memory where one
day you can look into the camera and say we won the war
and I proudly served but didn't stay to savor the victory.

John still tests white lightning the old-fashioned way and
what a signal he can give when the brew is ready.

John May

When Wilson Knew to Fold

Of all the familiar oddities his card-playing pals
had come to accept (like he always had to sit facing
the kitchen), it was a little peculiar when Wilson was
dealt a full house. Despite what he thought, he was
basically unlucky at cards.

He was known for his flash-quick temper during
regular Saturday night poker games at Jessie's,
where he would get the one-hand hot streak
of a win and swipe the table clean of his winnings,

Wilson Hensley

only to lose it all a couple of hands later. You didn't
call him any names if you wanted to avoid his wrath
especially when you called his hand and he refused
to fold. He considered himself the model of how

to finesse one's way around draw, stud, and low-in-
the-hole, this last of pokers he made up to show
them how proficient he was in the art of the bluff.

But that was how you played poker in those days:
using eye contact, hand gestures, and vocal
clues to either signal a win or conceal some clever ruse.

He was a shark among the mackerels and he knew
when to bite or when to pass. That is how one
plays. He never wrote any of this down.

I Am an American Rifle

"Lord of the Woods" I am called
among other fine words, including
"Constantine of the Universe." My
strength is grander and more beautiful

than any offering of nature as you can
plainly see by looking at the background.
They are the grandest of the grand displayed
with startled looks as if they had not

expected to end quite the way they did.
See the ghost of smoke rising from the barrel
before it reaches their eyes causing them to weep

Look at the lowly human how he cradles
me so firmly like I was a treasured offspring.
I am his hunter and he is my quarry. See
me dozing in the crook of his arm.

I am that special.   That scary.

T. W. Mundy

Where the Good People Are

Pick any morning by any semi-known river by an even more unknown rural town. Stand in the doorway of your local clothing store; watch for the country folk who will come down from mountains or rise out from hollows. You may not see them at first, but as sure as the sun rises over Swift Run they will come.

McGuire's Grocery will awaken as Eula unlocks the screen door and Edwin will begin to refill the cases with meats and fresh produce. He will gather up boxes for home deliveries and will struggle his enormous bulk into the pickup truck and as the springs make their weary complaint off he will go.

Mrs. Rouse will watch for his familiar face come up her driveway as she plans her weekly meals, some for her and Jack, some for her boarders which on any summer day of the '50s may include Blue Sox baseball players hoping for a national team call-up. On Saturday or Sunday afternoon the ballpark will open as the social magnet of the town where girls dress in pastel blouses and cropped slacks hoping to catch the eye of one of the players, all of whom are handsome, only one, or two, of whom is actually available as a boyfriend, and most of whom are totally thinking about baseball.

Back across the creek and into town we can take a quick inventory of standing buildings as it is not hard to do. They worked hard as purveyors of dry goods and commissioned bomb shelters but in their own paths of resistance managed to stay aloof. In their present day states they are as dry and barren as the old hotel's vine-choked swimming pool; and speaking of which, the Gables Hotel was the sight of all sights for those who considered the town a sought-after railroad tourist destination. Likely the exploits of Stanford White didn't make it any more notorious than it already was.

Keys to special rooms held prohibition liquors and rooms were set aside for selected paying guests and nameless visitors of the working classes, if you know what I mean. For theatrical events of the more plebian orientation the Elkton Theatre hosted such dignitaries as Gabby Hayes, Gene Autry, Tex Ritter, and Lash LaRue. Today the curtains are long tattered dresses and probably the screen is long gone full of holes from varmints of the mammalian variety. Sunsets have long ridden off.

Continued

The local clothing store anchors by an alley where at the backend of it, the jail stands. During the week it is mostly empty but come the weekend it is happily filled with those mostly needing to sober up and a few who need some patching up. Their moans and laments are always heard on Sunday mornings outside the merchant's loading dock as he works his books and figures out his next round of pictures. See, I am now telling the secret of this poem. This merchant was a kidnapper. He had a metal box fitted in such a way as to shoot people, hold them flat in a dark space, until he brought them back to life with chemical infusions and trickery of light.

In this poem I now reveal that the town was more than its buildings which as housings were nothing so special as to ever hold sway over the endurance of the people who lived there. The streets and storefronts were nothing more than façades, like window dressings; for they could mask the contents, and if we didn't know these people whom he photographed we would never know that within those structures there was breathing, living, laughing, bickering, crying, loving, and fighting.

Look for a man or a woman, any good man or woman and set them in the town among flowers and alongside curbs. Don't worry that the flowers seem fake and the concrete is cracked and torn out in spots. Watch these folks as they parade in and out of stores, dwell in company of their choosing, drink fully and deeply of choice spirits, gather on the seventh day in houses to beg forgiveness; these will be the ones we know and these are the ones who last after the sunset's long shadows have given us rural purity on the western slopes' horizon. There are still a few around who remember when their picture was taken and when he would position them in the right spot for the right amount of light. He and the rest are not gone.

They are just dead.

The Cisco Kid

He dreams of wild wests,
sorrelled ponies,
cowboyed boots and
prairied homes where
ranged voices sing of
fun, Momma, Papa.
In his sleep, toy guns
will slay the monsters.

He will never have to
grow up, but he does.
And when he looks back
on his life he will see it
reflected on shiny black
boots astride a faithful
rocking horse traveling
millions of miles under

a mulberry tree.

Robin Babington

Rocket Man

He'll smack that ball so far
it won't be found   at least on earth.

He'll outrun the bases so far
no measure will exist that can
frame the hit   at least on earth.

How he felt in those white flannels
and blue socks grasping that bat
must have been a spectacular
sensation on that day   at least on earth.

Home plate idles at his feet.
It cannot travel like the ball.
Not like him   at least on earth.

"Dee" DeArmond

Heroic Measures

You had to get past his good looks
if you wanted to hear his stories.
You couldn't sit there like him,
admire his smooth hair   impish smile.

You had to listen when he talked
to get the true humor of how he
would run cars off the road   cause
ladies to swoon   animals to
stampede   do all kinds of things.

You had to know he could take
anything he wanted   make
everyone and everything the better
for it   his trusty knife waving like
a banner up and down the streets.

He was king all right.   We all
loved him for it.   Such is hero worship.

Floyd Brill

Altitude

Young boys on the way to men
start out this way: it begins as
dreams for big things like
Navy pilots   big ships   alpine
heights   the immeasurable
scales of the imagination.

Anchored by time they
work on bikes   on flying
wagons   on tractors. Anything
to connect to the moving
with their borrowed tools.

When all these are lined up
a perfect order will emerge.
Dreams will converge and
evolve into the place they
always felt they knew.

Any postponement is brief.

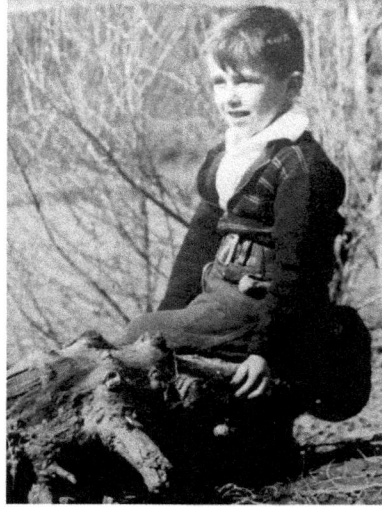

G. K. Lough

If It is Your Name

What's in a name, you may ask?
As if two "fs" and two "ts" describe
them rather than their prowess
with baseball. Fs for fouls
and Ts for tips. All hands at bats.

Two young boys, gloves on hands,
wait with no small amount of patience
for their turn in the field and on base.
They will do their share to keep the
runners on the bags, all the while

waiting for their own turns to knock
the ball out of the park. And isn't
that exactly what any young boy would
want to do in the summer of the lazy
days and dandelion fields? Listen

for the crack of ash. Field the white
leather-wrapped round core of solid
rubber. Then repeat. Swing. And repeat.

Larry and Garland Shifflett

Eyes in Flight

Fanciful flights. Immensity of vision
can converge in one man but only
if he believes all this happens in human
mortality. He soars above all he loves

and those who love him must stay
firmly planted on earth at his feet.
His gentle steps climb heights in
his imagination and take him beyond

mountains and to the world. He
wants to see everything and experience
it all. To feel and see brilliance. One
day he will before he touches down to earth.

He'll set his sights on those who came
to know him. He will bring them worlds
they can see, if only in books or on
little street corners. In their vision

everything will be big and wonderful.

Garner Downey

The History of Currency

He was considered wise in many of the world's ways
and there were those who may have called him crafty.

But he drew wisdom and possibly magic from the realms
of coins. More than collecting he felt the age and texture

of cast metallic currency and what these round solid discs
could say about a nation   or a man.

Impassive sovereigns hold no more action when left on
a table but in the hands of wise men can change history,

forge destinies and families, creating the path of humanity
across all countries and foreign lands only to wind up

in little villages, in the smallest of places, where one coin
can buy more than coffee.   It can buy a history.

Robert Lough

Italian Artwork

Somehow you knew he was the master carver
of hindquarters. His square Italian body type

exuded a confidence which came paired with
finely honed carving knives which he kept

lined up and ready by the meat case. Each
movement was a master stroke and each

smile when you placed your order was
returned in the same precision as if his

face had been finely carved into the
exact lines that describe a smile and

exact lines that twinkled his eyes when
you oohed and aahed over that special

rib-eye he had set aside just for you.
And didn't you know how lucky we

were that he set up shop in our little
town when with his good looks, his

precisely-parted black oiled hair
and his powerful hands which we

all longed to touch, we wondered
what it would be like to be stroked

even maybe carved by him realizing
it would somehow be an honor to be

that loved.

Owen "Buddy" Bruce

Knock It Out of the Park, 1955

About sixty years ago
Valley Blox tow-headed crew-cut
boys, lined up ready to play ball,
first had to pose with crossed arms
full of impatience to get to the bat.

In whatever they called formality
they held in laughter with molten
energy they had rather spend
on base running and gum chewing.

Little League - June 27, 1955

Ah, the smell of June grass hits
late day air along with the smell
of whitewood ash sticks having been
ignited by sparks flying off a spit-fire
fastball sending runners round the bases.

Sounds of come baby, come baby
rise out of bleachers and dug-outs
as players and fans pull against gravity
to get ten-and twelve-year-olds to break
the sound barrier and tag home plate.

Sixty years later while many of
those pictured have long left the park,
we still see and hear them laugh,
cracking jokes about how much they
love life, can't wait to play in the next one.

Making Music

When in the little town theater we meet up with faces of music,
we no longer feel we are in this tiny place as the theater seems
big, strong, everlasting, in other words, immortal.

Johnny and the boys could take us anywhere we wanted to go
in our minds simply strumming the strings. Our lives were
transported on high notes and smooth tenors singing out

stories of hardscrabble lives   broken hearts   unending
dreams of love   good drink   good friends   the kind that
would take you home after a hard drinking night   wash

your face with cool spring water telling you all the time how
much you were loved   how you saved that wreck of a fellow
who was bound and determined to kill his girlfriend that night.

Yes, it was that band whose breakdowns played along the banks of
the river and while both kept moving only one of them
really stayed. And we were always glad in those days.   Glad.

Ernest Berry, Wayne Hoak, Johnny Berry, Roosevelt Merica & James Meadows

Bat Boy

The noiseless trajectory of a spinning sphere
launched from an elevated mound some
sixty feet and inches away from home plate
is simply another blip on a youngster's
future radar screen.

Too small as a child to calculate necessary
physics he will wait his turn knowing there
will be many times at bat and many times
to run whether at the ball field or rounding
life's transparent bases.

He'll take the pitches, he'll check his stance,
look at the scoreboard, kick some dirt off
his spikes, and knock them all out of the park.

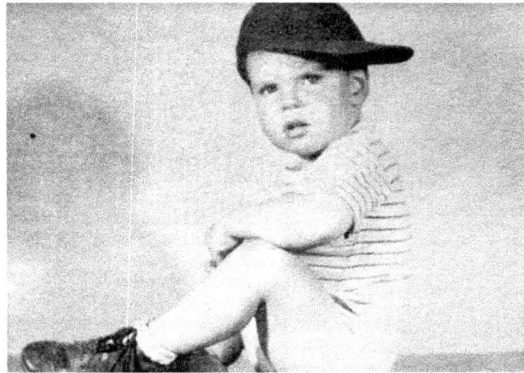

Bruce Thomas

The Barber of the Ville

Many truths are told in barber chairs
released by comfort in black leather.

Tales of deceit, conceit, and fanciful
pursuits can twist around striped poles

as if hatched from various powders and
colognes which keep guard within ear

shot on close-by shelves. The ordinary
talk can transform into whimsical

personalities only to be forgotten once
the right trim is achieved and towels

withdrawn. The humble craftsman looks
with pride at yet another successful shave

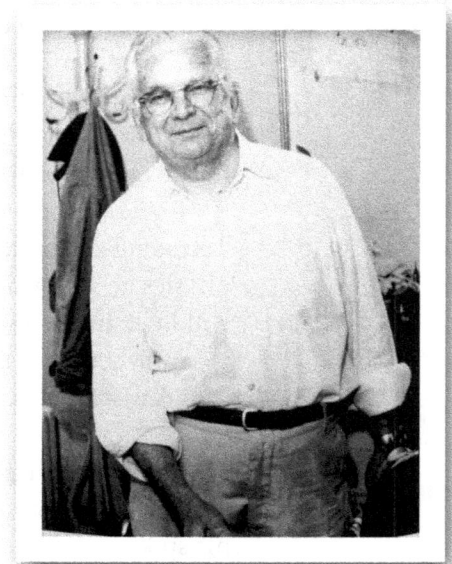

Joe Lucas

knowing that in a few days more truths
will return and again he'll cut and comb

in respectful silence while he waits, perhaps
longs, for another juicy tale, another fabrication.

But then who knows what is the truth
and what is not. He smiles as he always does.

Blends and Nature

We must not put our good nature to tests. There
are enough chances to fiddle with our mettle
without adding more acts and pretenses. Sometimes
enough is quite enough.

What if we were all mixed up into a large cosmic
blender designed to mold humanity into one
homogeneous clay? Nothing left to chance.

No takers on bets of the outcome, I imagine.
We would have to wait and see what happens.
Patience is a virtue.

But I will take that bet: we would pour out of this
fragile vessel onto all the lands and edges of seas
where we would look better—more human—kindly even.

Robert Lanier

Why Buildings Don't Talk

I think I am in Elkton and it would help
to know for sure. My concrete base is fixed
on this wide street and my flapping wings
hug a narrow alley which bears a very strange
name, someplace in the Middle East, I believe.

The bricks and mortar fixed in standard shapes
define the perimeters of the living and the inanimate
and within walls I could hear sounds like mythical
sirens calling to souls sailing by, daring not to glance
too longingly into windows. The people were like
cliff swallows diving and swooping around awnings
and doors seeking out other swallows or perhaps
a perch from which they could observe their world.

There were those days when I woke each morning
my mouth opened wide to receive and to shout stories
and salutes across the street to my dear friends who shouted
back and sent over waves and waves of new
voices, high and low, which continued through-
out the day. At least they used to when she
was a little girl and The Store was a cornerstone

of her life. Then my brick shirt was only missing
a button or two and I still stood grandly and quite
handsomely beside the street. But now I am missing
more than a few buttons. I am missing my teeth and
my tongue. My silence is unbearable but no one

is around to fill me up. I stand here starving and
crying alone, missing much of all that I knew. Maybe
someday someone will come back bathe me with
new colors, fill me to the top of my flat roof with
laughter and cries of joy. Until then I wait. I must

wait. That is what I now do best. It is always what
I was good at. Waiting. I may outlast it, but I
don't know for sure. She doesn't stop to look at
me anymore. I am that unbeautiful. I am that unearthly
now. I am that hollow inside. She doesn't see me.

But I still breathe. I still hear. Come closer.

Robinson's Department Store, 2015

Ghost Stories

Was the house haunted as a young boy believed?
Voices from embattled soldiers wondering why
they were camped here after a rough campaign.

Sounds of heavy boots clatter about on floor boards
which creak and groan, weighed down by armaments
and wounds still filled with spent lead and dirt.

Scratchings against walls from rough woven wools
and barely finished leathers can be heard over
snores of later peaceful residents. These noises

are ignored—settlings of timbers and cements it is agreed.
Listen. Quiet. Now. A pen drops. Ink dries. Blood clots.
Eyes blink. All are ghosts here.

Miller-Kite House (Stonewall Jackson's Headquarters)

What I Did For Love in 1969

What did I love about them?
I'll start with the drive beside the river. It's
the northbound route and straight as a ruler. I'm
heading home in the afternoon and you can pick
the year. Anytime between '69 and '79 will work
fine. I love the drive—it's a process, more than
arrival. In the anticipation I feel in the final 30 minutes
before pulling into the driveway, I'm prepping for
seeing my mother in her pink sweatshirt and moccasins.

Just like honing a knife, I fine-tune my attitude for
the greeting at the door. I will look eager, happy, but
not too much. Mom will, of course, invite me in,
offer coffee or maybe I'd rather a Coke. I'll take
coffee and yes I still drink it black. Your father is
at the store and I reply I'll go down in a little while.

We gather ourselves in the living room and start
the usual visit ritual. Doing fine. Doing fine, too.
Seeing anybody special? Nobody worth mentioning.
Your father and I are doing okay, too. We're older now
so we've forged our routines. Mine. His. Less ours.
That seems to work I say as I see a stain on her sleeve.

Mom says she'll work her Boggle letters for awhile
until suppertime. I go down to the store to check on
Dad. He's working acrostics between the one or two
customers he sees. I notice shirt boxes are the same
ones as the year before and probably the year before that.
Yes, I'm doing fine. He's doing fine. He's worried about
my mother. She doesn't seem herself. But then we are
growing older. He sold a couple of books earlier. It
comes and goes, you know. Sometimes people want
a book, sometimes they want to talk. Yes, I agree that
is true as I notice his left shoe has worn a hole.

Continued

After she died, he looked through closets and in dresser drawers.
Sometimes people miss someone. They go looking for
that person. Not sure where. Not sure why. But they do.
He wanted to find something. He never did.

It's a process. Like me driving home. After these years.
Not sure why. But I feel them, I really do, as I feel my eyes start to fill.

The Pride of the Girl Scout Cookie Promotion

Her dreams of girlhood
were revealed in an
unexpected smile—a
neatly pressed green uniform
spoke of convention lost on
the youngster whose wish for
recognition was simple: to be loved
for one moment, a moment like no other
thin mint that ever tasted so good.

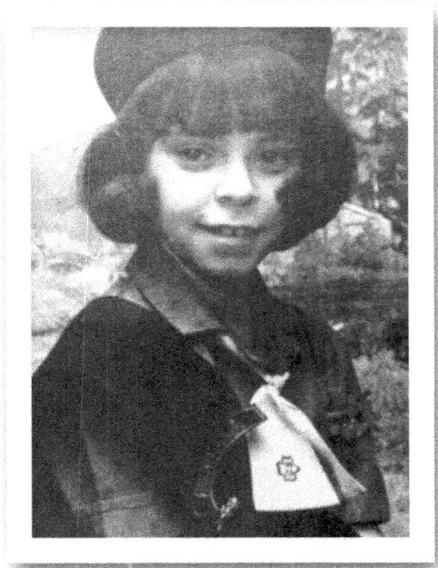

Tony Johnson

Supernova

Your surprise.   Your laugh
could not have been broader.

Eyes wide open with
amazement in the joy

of physics (which you did not know)
like supernovae,

brilliant creations where
all light startles. And we

caught up in the same flash
with our eyes wide open,

ready to be consumed,
find we can only laugh   too.

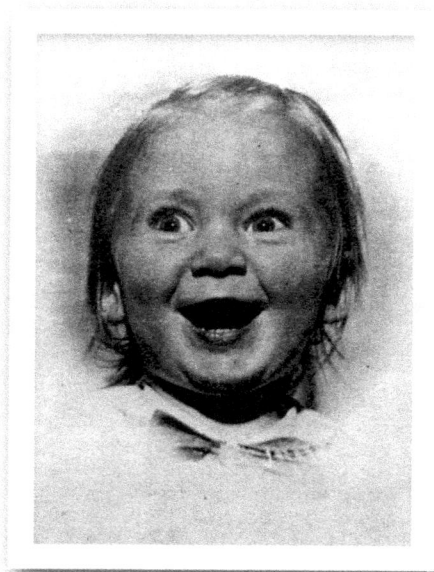

Carol Lee Brill

Good Girl

I can do anything.
All I want   I can do.
My Grandma lets me.

I parade between yards:
baby torso and chubby legs
that can run away and away.

Watch me   Watch ME:
   make mud pies
   pull the cat's tail
   teach her parakeet to say "Damn"
   pull up her tulips
   write some verse (in the pantry
      by flashlight   eating cake)

And she will say   "Good Girl."

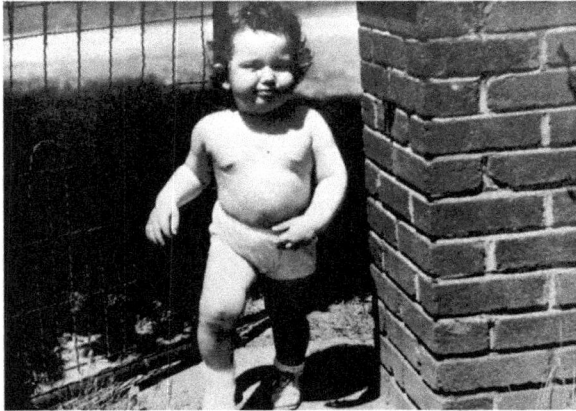

Sara M. Robinson

Pennies

If you will sit for me
and give up a smile,
I'll pay you well to wear
that coat I've set aside
for this very moment.

I have pennies you can keep.
Oh, you have to leave?   Then
take all that you brought.   I'll

keep the smile.   You take
the coat.   I'll keep the
three pennies that fell.

"Kim" Hensley

They are shiny: like new
like you.   You will break hearts

someday,   leave pieces
like tossed coins to roll away.

You won't miss them either.

A Dress of Balloons

Against the thistles, alongside
dandelion-seeded heads, she squirms—
complains, but nevertheless all agree
to pose. Grass is silent. Flag is sublime.
Only she squints against July sun.

Tennis shoes and scarf compete for
summer endurance and soon she
will outgrow even them. But she
will not outgrow this moment.
To bask in her own independence—
It is hers, thorns and all.

Teresa Fisher

All You Have To Do Is Imitate a Bird Call

You remember how birds sing, right?
You can improvise: a toot or a trill might work.

If you hear a cricket by the front door,
let him in for we need a lot of good luck.

If you hear the wood thrush sing by
my window, give him extra seed.

I want to hear all the sounds and songs
of nature. I know there are more than I

can ever love or ever want. Just the same,
I can try to warble and when I finally learn

maybe a few birds or animals will know
it is for them and will call me back.

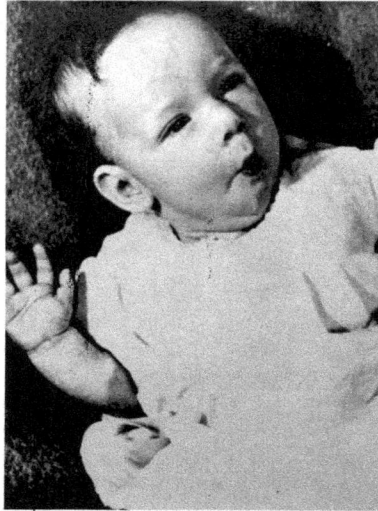

Jane Hammel

I Think I Can, But Tell Me One More Time

When you get your cake, you must eat it, too,
  but relish the moment when you do.

Don't take your journey too much to heart.

Don't form your disposition too much in advance.

Don't flee from hot spices that might light your life.

Don't be afraid to tell a dumb joke.

Don't take a wooden nickel from a stranger.

Don't ever buy a used pick-up truck from a relative.

Jeff Nash

As long as you are smoking, excel at exhaling the
  perfect smoke ring.

It is never too late to learn to swim, but it is always
  too soon to drown.

Keep searching.

Ricky

The parakeet said everything, just not complete
sentences. He offered prized words confined
to the decencies of his cage or from a stately
perch on her head.

He dared not test his wordsmithing on strangers
but every so often he goofed and you could hear
a lovely "damn" come from over the stove. Not

to be confused with the shouts from her grandmother
as she fussed over her daily preparations,
Sharon still would run every time a "shit" came forth.
It was too exciting to miss the perfect elocution.
He always hit the mark!

Life is too short for only pretty words.

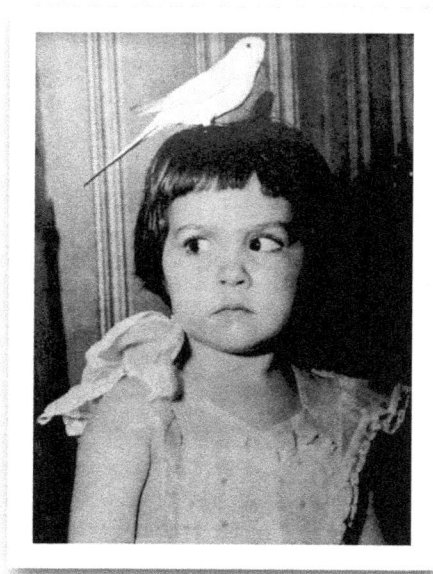

Sharon Whitlock

The Elkton Deluxe Pool Hall

Chatter rings like no other when
the cue ball breaks the perfect rack
into stripes and solids careening
against felt, falling into leather pockets.

Run the table shouts leap over bar stools,
beer bottles and scattered currencies as
the young boy sweeps merrily towards
the front door. He has a secret you know.

He's at home here amidst the smoke and
scents of grease and blue chalk. He knows
every move and has memorized each inch
of the table edges. Later after the hall is

closed he'll pick up his favorite stick, lean
against the east side of the table, whisper
I can take them all.

Joe "Buddy" Hammer

Blue Sox

There is no such thing as an un-handsome ball player.
Our genetics protocol has an underground agreement
with the fixers of DNA. The creators of athletic genomes
have kept this secret from us for many years

(maybe since the beginning of baseball).

From their carefully secured bunkers amidst test tubes, striped
socks, and tons of graph paper, they've noted trends
and kept statistics, such as hair color, shoulder widths,
height, weight, facial features(ah, yes, lips and blue
eyes). They didn't forget hands either: perfectly shaped
for the glove. Knuckles shaped to bend along baseball seams.

We see them then.   We see them now.   We want them
more than ever to play ball and slide safely into home.
Another safe play and stolen bases for good luck and good looks.

Blue Sox, 1952

A Fine Day for Love

You have to hand it to the kid,
there is a lot to be said for cuteness.

There is not enough of it these days.
We are missing something about

innocence and trust and believing
that someday a person can grow

up, fall in love, and live a good life
that in itself can be rendered cute,

as in delicate and classy, as in describing
what is delicate and lasting,

someday will take more than a simple
one-syllable word. It will mean

that love is the best of everything.

Kenny Shifflett

Snapshot of Perfection

Perfection is more than expertly placed creases in a striped summer dress. It is more than delicate fingers which grace countertops and packages. It is more than watching others smile in spontaneous reply to hers.

It is more than hearing her ask all those who entered: what are your wishes? what can I reveal for you? I can harness wind and gasps of countless souls who happen to gaze.

Her eyes offer up promises of summer and we hear birds sing praises. We can only return soft murmurs of assent, some small sacrifices which are trivial but all we have.

Her beauty pours out and washes over us; she a purifying waterfall: speaking quietly, and at once. We as thirsting pools.

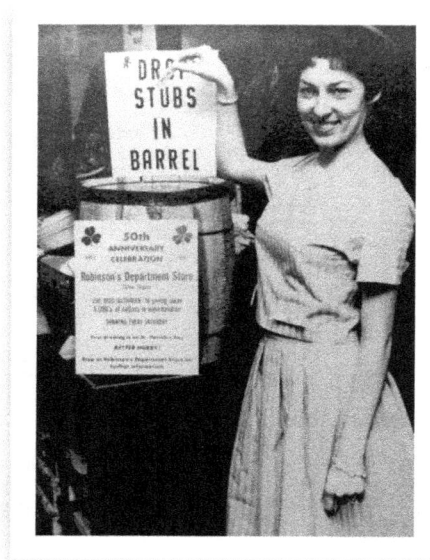

Hilda Jenkins Snow

Wedding Day

A well-dressed man with no flaws noted has
last bits of lint swiped by his friend. Preparations.
For today he is the prince of perfection and ambassador
of love.

All elements have aligned with utmost labor designed
with no small amount of tension and a huge amount
of electrical current.

Now the day has arrived where some at least can rest,
but this is merely the beginning. Ceremonies

will commence and for the man and his future bride
joy will arrive, carried in a carriage of its own light
on strong shoulders: his best man and him, the knight.

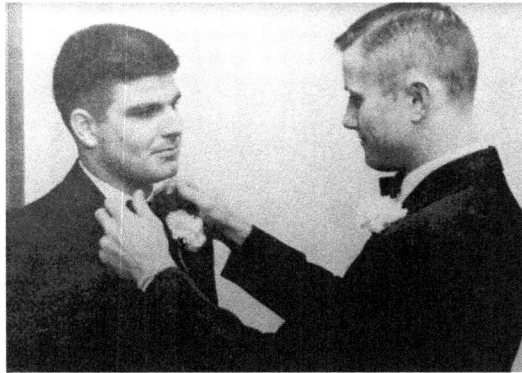

Philip Secrist and Elmer Lam

His Hat

There are some basic facts about men
among others who reside on this side of
"the Ridge:"

We spell our last name with 2fs and 2ts
so you know what parts we are from.

We tame our straw hats and then we
wear them til they die.

We smoke ourselves to death and then
live to tell about it.

We have a smile that drives the girls
crazy.

We wouldn't leave here or change
our name for nothin'.

Marshall Shifflett

I Can Spell

I can spell incarnation—
it is what I know because
when I wake up every morning
my momma says I am a living
incarnation of every flower that
grows in our back yard. She says
I am brighter than the dandelions
and sweeter than the pansies.

See me as a recapitulation of
who I will be a short while
from now.

I am a pretty little girl and someday
when I am all grown up a special
someone will say I am the living
incarnation of her.

I can't wait.

Terry Levinson

Distant Cities

Is not every small town
the guilt of every large one?
The large town the guilt
of the city?

Who withdraws from the
streets they love? Only to
find their footsteps tread
over steps of those who

paced back and forth
over decades, maybe
generations, in the same
place never leaving far

from yards where the
horseradish grew next
to white fences and the
cockscomb strutted

beside cracked walks.
Innocence seemed forever
but was lost every time
a stranger arrived and

told of places away and
even further away that
were larger with more
people who one would

never notice.

It's a Place and It's a People

It is a place unlike most others except when
you leave you can return but you cannot come back.
It is a town of its own time-warp creation and while
people and buildings age, fall apart, and develop
the weathered skin of being outdoors too long; on
the other hand nothing much changes.

For many of us time stopped in the particular year
in which we left. For me it stopped in 1965, only to
start again, stop again, start again, every time I came
up the north-south road.

The mountains have changed where some homes are
now built on mountainsides. The river is the same, though,
and maybe one run out of two is the new rule. I think
sometimes I am afraid of changes. These mean

some things will get lost or forgotten. It's the people:
so many of them in such a little place. They are their own
world, and in my quiet moments when I write, I think of them
knowing they haven't changed at all. They stopped right

where they were supposed to, and I am still going. I can
see the river moving. It will always take time with its
gentle washing of   banks   grasses   rocks   sounds.

There Are Linewomen in Our County

What a new power—more than electric lines
which cross our county and connect all other
counties and connect us to the world.

What a new power that came from
equality of work fairness between men
and women which was more than a wish.

What of this do we want? No distractions
no discouragement, but accepting all sleeplessness.
    Sore bones   wearied hands   heavy hearts
We know what we must endure in the name of equality.

We cannot be lost within our new power. Our grid
cannot be silent. We are not lost and we are not
reflections. When we climb, we rise higher.

Carolyn Williams Frank

Bonita

Before she was "Bonnie" she was "Bonita,"
when I was in high school and she was
as tall as a tree.

She had a flawless overhead set shot
and I worshipped her ability to handle

the big round ball on any court in any gym.
She was a giant in the sport when there
were few women who played like her.

Her smile was a magician's locket moving
back and forth and with her laugh she
could coax ticks off a barn dog,

in any weather   infallible   tireless.

Our champion.

Bonita "Bonnie" Comer

Lam Family Gives Us Bluegrass

When they sat to play on church grounds
it wasn't about getting the notes going
or the words running.

It was about sitting and playing and you
could hardly expect to see sheet music
or music stands.

Verses and tunes were already composed
in heads. Nothing else to do, but to do it.
Give it up for the Almighty and a few others

while they are at it. Baritones and soprano
mixed with catgut strings and hand-carved
wooden picks would herald the perilous inferno.

As we sat watching them assemble their art,
one might ask when they started: what key
are all ya'll in?

Don't matter, they would say.
Just sing it like it is.

Lam Family Singers

Stihl Life with Zeke

Outside the town,
inside the dump,
day after day he
shoveled remains of
his little town.

He was a mayor of sorts—
ranger of his domain,
astride his steel carriage
lifting and sorting
packing and heaving.

He could tell you all
you ever wanted to know
about buildings and their
internal shiftings.

You could read between
the lines on his face and
the cigarette in his hand
more than anyone should
probably know.

Scant shade under his work
hat provided his only cover

for he moved mountains
everyday. Some was dirt.
Some clung. Some fell off.
Some was rich. All was real.

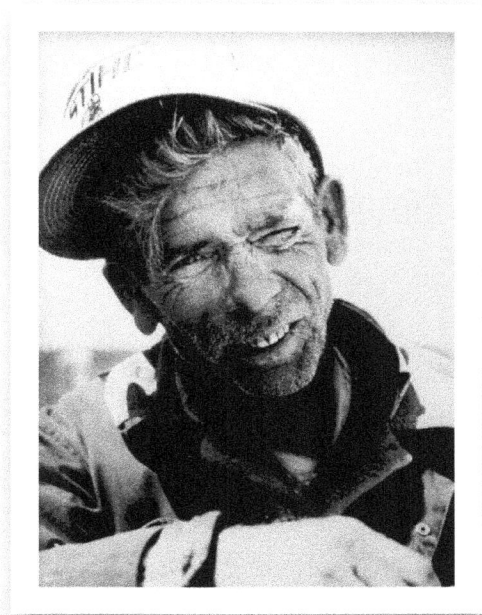

Charlie (Zeke) Baugher
(Photo by Nita Cole)

Hobby and Buddy Talk the Truth Down by the River

Summer
Two town icons
Photographer and insurance salesman
Pro-lifers (as in they lived in this town all their lives, pro-fessionally)
Elktonians of the first degree
Standing and smiling by waters of life
(As brought to you in bottles and cans for your future
enjoyment by your local beer brewery)

Drink and think responsibly, preferably not alone
and always when the world is calm, especially
during summer nights when grass is green with
meadows full of chirps so loud that their
wisdom is grander than your own.

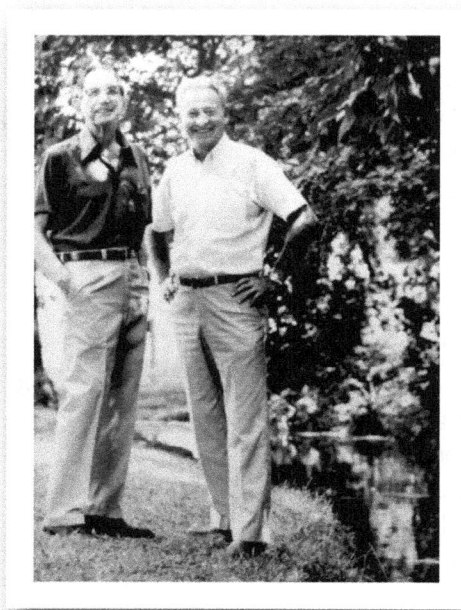

Hobby Robinson and Buddy Workman

Southerner Defined

From the middle pages of a Faulkner southern gothic
rose this persona of gentility who in his relaxation
was so perfect (in that southern kind of way) that
the very porch he sat upon quietly thanked him
for sitting there.

Bees stopped their gathering…
Plants paused in their flowering…
Paint stopped its drying…
A white mustache stopped its growing…

All this so a kindly southern gentleman could
think on how a morning of the seventh day
could be so quiet   so restful   so patient.

Mike Harrison, Sr.

Shuttlecocks

Pretty little birds in summer plumage
with finely sewn satin dresses—puffed
at the shoulders and printed with
stripes in every direction—attempt to fly.

It's a big world for a bunch of young
fledglings testing their wings which seem
to be formed as all left ones.

They lift a little here, touch down a little there;
confuse directions out of the nest and land
in the middle and on the edge.

Then turn around and do it all over again.
Flying from each side of the earth takes
imaginative feathering and many tricky landings.

The "Rockettes" of Elkton
"Don't look down, don't look down!"

American Heracles

I, too, am America – Langston Hughes

I have inhaled the spice of shoe polish
and dreamed of my future.
I sat at the feet of treasured uncles who
taught me history, and then another history.

I played in corn fields and rode buses
seeing first hand the country where
I was born.
I missed no windows...

I took my strong spirit and flew away
from here leaving my family, only
to return on occasion for funerals.
I missed no windows, no doors.

I have taught in universities and I
have a family, a car, a house, bills,
and all those consequences and
incidentals of being America.

I have missed no windows, no doors and
through each one life has not passed me by,
nor has any winter chilled my bones.
I see over any snow. I have outrun the sun.

Don Banks

SS Hillman

Whether to fame or infamy,
ships leave safe harbors taking
those aboard to foreign ports.

Within their walls cargo shifts
and settles among workers and
philosophers who'll emerge late

in a day voicing wisdom hidden
in menus and setting next to countertops,
washed against salt shakers and

imported coffee cups. Secrets become
news served with rare prime rib and
cherry smashes. Gravy covers a little

truth and bread breaks all the words
down then softens them with butter.
We could never get full.

The ship never sank. It just returned to port
where it listed slightly to starboard.

Ship's Crew at the Famous Battleship "Hillman's Elkton Restaurant"

Jeddie Paints the Town on Ben-Yehuda Road

Where else in this land, at least in this valley,
okay, let's say this town, would you expect
to find a master painter like him?

He has now solidified his fame by painting
the most famous road in the world and he
didn't have to leave the state.

Art resides in his soul and weeps pigment
through his fingers so that every color he
touches has his force of life within.

From an old torn-down hotel to vistas
around the meadows and mountains he
has wept graciously, spread his gifts, and

turned everything to magic.

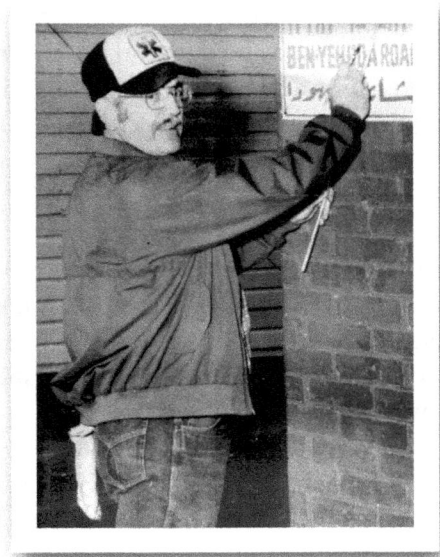

Jeddie Hensley

The River Always Gets the Last Word

And the river kept its babbling over and over. Saying the same things,
like when we would buy beer in Shenandoah   water ski on its backside
right in front of the dam. Sure we were daring it to pull us over   watch our
flailing arms and legs go   careening off the sides of the banks   cartwheeling over rocks
laughing at ourselves. The river. The boys would laugh too at
us. I was so awkward. Margie was so pretty. It was wonderful that the

river kept talking. We kept talking, drinking National Bohemian.
Being the renegades that we were, I told my mother I was spending the
afternoon on the river with some friends. She was impressed.
The river is still yakking: take what you want, like when my father caught
crayfish for bait under the trestle, fished for hours for bass, tried to forget the yellow
convertible.

When I would drive over the river, in my little green Crosley,
the hood would fly up. I had to reach out over the tiny windshield and
hold that plastic plate of a hood down, with a couple of fingers. It was so tiny

and thin. The river would be chuckling below me. As I drove into town
in my little car, having turned around in one lane at the town limits,

I couldn't escape quite yet. I always headed back   with the river
always laughing at me   forecasting my future   like it knew exactly
how it would go   or not, like when the little green car was hung up
the high school flag pole, while I was acting out my life in the junior class play.

I knew I would eventually leave, my father having sold the poor little thing. All the
while the river still hums
                    moving a few rocks.   Nothing ever sleeps   around here.

The Gables

It was impossible to curtsey for her
even though she was the grande dame,
set upon the never-ending lawn which
backed up to the never-ending river.
She welcomed royalty with a blush
as she was fixed onto the ground
about as fast as the concrete which held
up her mighty bosoms.

*The Gables Hotel
Opened 1891 - Razed 1957*

Washed by sunlight and perfumed by
river breezes the elegance of her style
overtook any and all who approached
her wide staircase. Even the richest
of men removed their hats upon her
greeting, and they did not expect as
much as a nod from the highest
porticos.

To put it another way she anchored
a town which became the fashion
runway for the tuxedos
and sequined dresses she attracted
as city finery touched down on shining
floors and shinier faces.

Watching on the sidelines were townsfolk
who listened to the orchestra on many a
Saturday night lift its music through
windows, across tables and dancers,
and out across the porch and lawns

where the loveliness was watched by
tear-filled eyes for something this grand
in this place, so unreachable.

The History of Bloomer Springs as

recounted by Lute Lam: who dares to
roar who am I? As if I care since I am old
now. My mule is blind and I'm jailed with
nothing left to lose or claim.

But I got this spring and I got this mountain
and you can't have 'em. My swole feet

filled with dirt between toes fill out these
rough wool socks and keep me upright to
look mayors and sheriffs eye-to-eye.

Yes'm.   I am Lute Lam and when you look
at me, look hard as you can for as long
as you can. As far as you can see
I am this land. I am this land.

Lute Lam

"Zut"

If one man on a horse defines a frontier
then let him come forth and give us
his ideas of boundaries. In return
we will mark all the edges with ploughs
and furrows and hay bales alongside
brick and planks and asphalt streets.

We will invite him into our town
and give him the homage he deserves
when he calls out to us that he
is the last remaining truth: he is
the last warrior we will ever know.
We will look into his ruffed face,
wrinkled grizzle, see his kindly eyes

and know that he speaks the truth.

Herman Zetty

Shine

Back in folded hills as curved as coils from old cars,
some distilling is going on alongside an exhausted little
creek. What these boys have found to do with branch
water is better than fishing for catfish and less smelly.
They take, from their own leftover crops, squeezings
and run clear liquid through miles of copper into and
out of bottles and through bags of charcoal.

We wonder at the potency of spirits in the bottles
and in the passing of the brew among them we know
that in a few years they could be blind but for now
they sip gratuitously the 200 proof of their whiskey
which I'll call "Old Overalls," out of respect since
they are not here to tell about it. But in that time

they had their dangerous fun, didn't they?

Blue Ridge Mountain Boys

The Naylor Sisters

Of the possible memorable families
these sisters wore their popularity
amid amazing bounty created by
hugging farmland and gardens
of cornucopia plentitude.

Posed in their foursome as the sun
squinted their eyes, they did not
attempt to smile as this was a serious
occasion. The traveling photographer
offered for a very small fee to take
a lasting portrait for the parents

whose later descendants would gift
the picture to a young man now
grown, who then waited eagerly
for their weekly arrival in the
store where he knew he could
sneak longing gazes at their
smart outfits and tucked waists;

all the while pretending to sort
out butter beans and grapes carted
in by the very protective father.

The Naylor Sisters

Canned Summer Heat

It is the end of summer and last
rites are held on a slow moving river
bank. It is the boys who are growing
amidst fish jumping, worms sliding,
crawfish running.

Men to boys, boys to men, the
endless cycle of how nature works on the
human side of things where tales
of extraordinary feats are used to
counterbalance the trivial acts that
boys seem to find amusing. But we
know, all the same, they need to try.

We wish we could take those years
with us in a portable container that
could be opened from time to time
in small lifts of a not-so-tight lid
to remind us that living on the edge
of a big world is not as scary as

tales told around the midnight camp-
fires when someone sneaked into
the woods to rattle sticks and make
soft snorting sounds. But then if we

open that can too many times we
risk losing all the memories of
summers of very long ago and we
risk the loss of absoluteness when
we need it the most.

Frog Island Boy Scout Camp

The Photographer in His December Labyrinth

For him December seemed a transformative month
  his honky-tonk tavern long ago shot itself in the
  foot and other places for the last time.
  He was about to be a father for the first time.
Then after years of hunting and gathering he
released his first book.

He was akin to Ulysses for his journeys
took a very long time and traversed a lot of
rough spots, not the least of which was his
marriage. But he was the hero of his self-made
epics and in his stops he documented all
he saw with his faithful companion named
Graflex. It was his Friday to his Crusoe, his
Watson to his Holmes; and in an ironic twist
perhaps consider Molly to his Leopold.

Hobby Robinson
December, 1969

His labors over for this first chapter he rested
and relived the sagas knowing full well he
was not finished. He would do this again and again.
He didn't accept the destination for long as
he was alive when he and his companion
were on the move. December for him was
the coldest month.

One Man Not Often Mistaken for Woody Allen

There are men like no other:
faithful   stoic   proud   alone.
They exist in some external
world but know nothing of life
beyond a small town's limits.

There are men who resemble
those of more fame   resolute
restrained   confined to some
province where they will not
expand beyond a water's edge.

There are men whose sounds
echoed in summer ballparks,
who measured lengths of coats
and flannels in winter store-
fronts where their world stopped

at a wooden door   heavy.
There are men like no other:
left   separated   from a beloved
twin   who must live for both
to dwell   in one place   one time

These are men worth talking about.

Ernie Herring

Master Woodcarver

Raising fiber out of a wood plank to create
a relief of such texture must come from some
notion that a human face will form from lines
and impressions.

Tools that carve must be an artist's hands to impart
humanism to such wood; for life will have to rise
as if summoned by special talents only held

by few who can take something as dead
as a wooden plank, and with care and patience
follow patterns. In one clarifying moment

at the end when he sets down the tools for the last
time pronouncing the rendering finished, he can
look up and see his issue has risen into the light.

Norris Shifflett

An Officer and a Guitar

Between arrests one way to calm
the tensions is to strum out an old
bluegrass tale about the one drunkard
who didn't like being in jail because
the food was just not to his liking.

An officer in his fine dress browns,
stogie fixed comfortably between lips,
hums out these few bars and thinks
about how he'll get up for his shift
in just a little while, but for now his

fingers are more at ease with the gentle
stroke on the D string than curled around
the trigger on his 45. He'd rather sit
and tune his guitar than chase out
speeders to the edge of town.

Seems to him that beating on a guitar
makes more sense than beating on
some ol' poor soul whose cries don't
carry a tune like he would prefer to hear.

Maybe in his dreams he would have
a banjo-picking girlfriend. Then he would
be living right. He would.

Officer Ernest Harrison

Stepping to Music

She watches his feet while he tenderly
watches her face. With a smoothness
usually seen on well-worn guitar strings,
he leads her to center stage and then
the magic begins.

Maybe you could say they were the local
pride of the jitterbug set or our own version
of dancing with the stars at the Twist and Shout.
But whatever you may want to call it, they were
tapping out rhythms more than fancy dance steps.
These were the steps of their lives.

Such was a special Saturday night when
music filled up a local club hall and laughter
flowed out the doors, bounced against
mountain walls, and returned to those inside,
who for brief moments felt that this life
was all anyone would ever need or want.

Cynthia Hensley and Shorty Stepp

Gods and Goddesses

Of the places and things that surround us,
of snow underfoot and bright sun penetrating
air and highlighting boy and girl figures,

He sent them all into the camera box through
the portal and onto a thin sheet of celluloid
where images rested until he gave them

life again. When they emerged these two—
young god and goddess—smiled at
how on that very cold day the outside

temperature was not nearly as important
as inside temperatures for they were
filled with the heat of youth and nothing

could stop them from creating their own
part of the sun.

Clyde Jenkins and Dixie Levinson

The Age of Innocence

Fidgeting on the tatting-covered chair,
two blue-eyed doll-baby girls giggled,
squirmed, and flirted with the over-
anxious photographer, eager to simply
get the session done.

They are the innocent. He is the master.
They are the prize. He is the door.
Behind the curtain of his flash will
emerge a shot, given to paper, that
will later tell stories of how innocence

can be found in the best places, but
only from watching evolution or
returning to scrapbooks with
fading yellow velox glossies.

Turning ghostly…leaving.

Marla and Vana Longley

The Secret That Was Betty

Would you linger a little longer
by the lilacs that frame the river?
Would you take on the scent of
an April blossoming and keep it
close to your heart always?

Gaze upon me all that you can—
spare not a wink or a smile
until eternity stops for all
the universe.

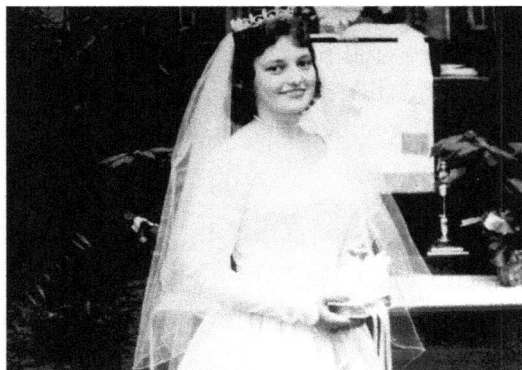

Betty Flick Secrist

These were the thoughts within
all who entered the store where
she clerked and if they could speak
poetry would have said out loud:

O, she walks as if she dances on air!

But they didn't and they couldn't—
for once they threshholded over to
aisles of shirts and jeans the only
hope they had was simply to be
seen by her. Waiting takes the words,

and in those inestimable moments
eternities come and they go.

Displaced

Deep   down low dark hollows.
Rocks as big metamorphic
gneiss: all the more
inaccessible, but prized
by those who would hear
their own voices echo from
those skarned boulders in
long evenings of long days.

The Breeden Family

Doming hillsides still slope gently
down to wandering creeks where
simple folks tapped unselfishly
at pure deep water   abundant fish.

Unlike crawfish which could hide
beneath the swirls   eddying stones,
these folks lived too exposed to remain
secreted into hollows   bottoms.

Their land too prized for access by a larger
public who would someday look over
these hills and valleys wondering aloud
as to who could possibly live there.

While some of us wondered who could
leave there.   Some did.   Some died there.

The rest disappeared from us.

Leaving Elkton

I cried, then sighed at their graves.
Deep in the earth, in their private little chambers,
I wondered if they heard me.

I came through on my way west.
Hardly recognized the town: empty streets, vacant lots.
Old storefronts hang around with nowhere else to go.

Drove past where I grew up. Glanced around the neighborhood.
I don't know anyone here.
Pressed for time, like I thought it mattered,

I headed for the cemetery. It was only a short…short detour.
A cemetery for a small town. My parents are there, in spots
reserved for them. I passed on mine.

No one thought I would return, now I'm passing through.
At their gravesites, I said some words, catching them up on my life.
I guessed they'd want to know, but I didn't expect any response.

Back in the car, back on the road, I hear my mother say:
   You come back soon now, you hear?
as I see the sun due west in front of the car.

If I speed up I might cross a state line before sunset.

   Before I hear her say it again.

About the Author

Raised in the little town of Elkton, Virginia, right in the heart of the Shenandoah Valley, **Sara M. Robinson** grew up amidst the townsfolk who her famous photographer father, Hobby Robinson, had captured on film and subsequently self-published in nine books. After graduating from college, she embarked on a career in sales, marketing, and product development in the chemical and minerals processing industries. She published prolifically and was granted a US patent as well. In 2009, she retired to begin a new life in creative writing. Her inaugural work, a memoir, titled *Love Always, Hobby and Jessie* was published in 2009. *Two Little Girls in a Wading Pool* (2012), *A Cruise in Rare Waters* (2013) and *Stones for Words* (2014) share her life stories and observations in poetry. Sara resides in Albemarle County near Charlottesville.

Index

(Poem Titles in **Bold**)

www.ingramcontent.com/pod-product-compliance
Lightning Source LLC
Chambersburg PA
CBHW081418090426
42738CB00017B/3411